21 Poems to Help Shy Job Seekers

Beth N. Barr

BookLeaf
Publishing

India | USA | UK

Presentation by *BookLeaf Publishing*

Web: www.bookleafpub.com

E-mail: info@bookleafpub.com

ISBN: 9789358315806

First edition 2024

ACKNOWLEDGEMENT

Thanks go to BookLeaf Publishing for this opportunity!

I want to thank my mother. It was her love of Victorian artwork and antique book collecting habits that introduced me, at a very young age, to the world of classic poetry. The visual beauty of ornately illustrated borders, on foxed pages within those antique books, communicated to me that there was beauty to be found within the words and their arrangement, also.

I'd like to share an excerpt from a poem that called out to me and sparked this love of poetry, in particular. I believe was from The Woodbine, Poems by Clara Loud (1861) and it was called, "The Language of the Eye."

"Love will not dare his power reveal,
Grief cannot language find;
The heart may bitterest anguish feel,
And yet vain words may blind.
Despair may e'en lie all concealed,
Tho' broken heart be nigh;
Save by one language 'tis revealed,
The Language of the Eye."

I want to thank my father, who fostered creativity in me as well, and lovingly supported my waxing and waning creative interests as I grew up.

I want to thank my loving husband also, whose eyes are like gorgeous, infinite pools, and I just love to lose myself in them. He has been so supportive of all my creative efforts over the years.

Ultimately thanks go to the Creator, for the creativity we all have as humans, our free will, and the full spectrum of human emotion together with the beauty around us that inspires what we call "the arts".

TABLE OF CONTENTS

Twenty-One

There's nothing like turning twenty-one and,
Just then realising, you don't know a thing
about…

Surviving among a forest of trees,
People who are taller, people who are smaller
and are…

Living in a world where love exists.
And you didn't see it.
Turning into dust and only just, so that,
Things make sense and you don't feel like
everyone else.
Life begins to get a little better, when you're…

Giving what you've got without being asked.
It doesn't take a lot to give love back.
But then, that is just what it's all about.

Cuz there's nothing like waking up and being in,
Love with life and living, yes that's when life
begins.

It's learning to turn into a friend whom,
Others can depend on, you…
Can't just hide or turn it off and on…

That's when,
You're twenty-one.

Just Another Day

It's an ordinary day for the examiner,
An ordinary day for the wind.

Just another day for the birdies in their nests...
They don't know the difference
between now and when I will have been on my
driving test, yes…

It's just another day for the examiner...
just another day for everyone.

Though it's every day that I do my very best,
this could be the day that I pass my test.... yet…

It's just another day for the examiner,

Just another day under the sun.
Just another day for waves over the sea...

…but it just could be THE day for me!

You Have It In You

I just remembered a happy thing
I was young, sick in bed with a cold maybe.

I remember my Mother
On bed's edge sat
Bending over to give
Me a kiss and at that,

Her beautiful, long hair
At the time, came loose,
It fell over, and around me
As a protective curtain, drawn closed.

It was a simple, so simple,
Yes, simply perfect moment.
A perfectly simple moment of simply perfect
happiness.

Apart from which,
I have no other.

And yet that's what I used to think.
I thought I had no happy childhood memories,
no joyous times to speak of.

Until Beth asked me, until somebody cared.

Until she said, "I believe you do.
Give it some time, it'll come to you. I just know
it's there."

I waited a day, then two, then three.
Then lo and behold it came to me.

If only I'd known sooner,
If only that joy could have sung its song,
And if only I'd believed
It was in me all along.

Roses Too Fine to Miss

Once in a while
I stop and I smile
At the smell of these here roses.

As gifts from above
Revealing gentle love
Soft and sweet, the petals show this.

All that you dream,
You chase like a wish,
Yet you might find
these roses too fine to miss.

How to be happy in the now?
Be thankful for who you have around.
Love the ones you love, yes do it now,
While they're here, while they can be found.

Take these roses, put them in a vase,
Keep them in your heart always.

All that you dream,
You chase like a wish.
Yet you might find
these roses too fine to miss.

Yes, take time out of your schedule.

Take these roses and keep them well.

Appreciate their precious smell.

Stop to hear their petals tell,
The fleeting goodbye kiss
of roses too fine to miss.

Advice From My Younger Self (20yr-self to my 40yr-self)

I hate to tell you,
But you've told me that story before.
Is it because you're older than me,
Or is it because you're becoming a bore?

When you start telling one of your favourites,
Do you go into performance mode?
Do the lights in the theatre hide the audience,
And you perform to a faceless crowd?

Do you not rely on feedback?
Do you not care whether they give you a sign?
That maybe you've told them this one before?
And that maybe you're wasting their time?

Next time turn those theatre lights around,
know they're not shining on you.
Look into the face of your audience,
Look for their interest, look for a cue.

Because even if you tell a story,
Remember it's not about you.

It's about something of value to the
person, the person you're telling it to.

And keep a journal of your stories.
And keep track of who you've told what.
So the next time people yawn, it won't be yours,
rather someone else's story, not making the cut.

The Day My Shy Was Born

When I was small
I liked to be
alone
And play with dolls

But I didn't mind
Others there with me.
I didn't mind at all.

I didn't like to put others out.
Didn't like to awkward seem.
Didn't like to have particular needs.
And yet I knew had them.

On one day in particular, these two sides of me
met.

They didn't get along at first, they seemed at
odds, and yet,

The two became one and then became torn.
And that was when my shy was born.

My need to feel free, with the need to others
please.

My need to be alone, with the need to be in a
team.

To find myself alone that day, with others' eyes
wide upon me,

As if in disbelief, disdain,
Their gaze caused a shame I could feel.

It was at school and I think,
I was five or six.
And we'd been given a weekend assignment.
We could work in pairs or work alone,
To invent a musical instrument.

To keep things simple for my parents,
I opted to work on my own,
And fashioned some bottles into a shape,
And took it to school Monday morn.

The teacher then said that was just the first part.
The second, was to now sing a song.

We'd each practice using the thing that we'd
brought,
then in front of the class sing it out.

As I saw other teams playfully perform each
their piece,

I started wishing I wasn't alone.
I'd chosen the song, The Mighty Jungle, for
some
crazy odd reason I'll never know.

After the first few "Awimbo-ways" I thought I
was doing ok.
But it was when I went "aweeeeeeeeee"
then I saw it, in their eyes, some kind of
disbelief.

Had I hit a wrong note?
Was I hurting their ears?
Do they think that I think that I'm good?

This internal dialogue was spiralling away,
even as I was singing "aweeeee", honest, it's
true.

And although unuttered, I am sure it was then,
that I promised myself, "Never again."

Yes, that was the day my shy was born.
Two sides of myself met, then were torn.

Safe Circles

Sometimes going in circles,
Gets a bad name, a bad rap.
When people get lost in the desert,
Going in circles becomes a death trap.

They've even studied this tendency,
Which shows up when we're lost in a forest.
So of all earth's creatures it seems,
Our sense of direction's the worst.

Or could it be, we can make a case,
For times when our circling can be good?
When coming back home, or starting again,
And thinking of would've, should've, could'ves...

Can actually help us re-centre ourselves
If framed in the very best of ways.
Yes, framed with a forward moving action plan
in mind,
to help us make changes, make gains.

And couldn't it be said that the planet we're on
Is constantly going round and round?
The moon, as well as the the water we drink,
Anywhere you look, nature's cycles are found.

The consistency of these, the stability they provide,
Enable us to make trips to outer space.
We can leave the safety of this particular 'comfort zone'
Trusting they'll still be here to re-embrace us.

Indeed, it's the stable circles and cycles,
And so called comfort zones of life,
That make it possible for us to venture out.
And taste things new, things that excite.

It's knowing we have them to come home to,
That gives us a deep sense of peace.
Remove them completely, and what do you get?
Life on this planet, well, it could cease.

Love is Multifaceted

Today I saw an interview,
An old one, with Lucille Ball.
The interviewer asked for her definition of love,
And stumped, she asked him for his, and all!

But it got me thinking, if I were asked,
What would I choose to say?
It took me while to gather my thoughts.
Then I simplified them, I hope that's ok?

It's not simple, not even ours to define.
Because love is multifaceted.
That's what I'd say its definition is,
If pressed, when someone asked me it.

The ancient Greeks had four words for it,
Familial, friendly, principled, romantic.
Paul talks about love in 1 Corinthians,
Almost like a dos and don'ts list:

"Love is patient, kind, and not jealous.
It does not brag or show off,
Does not become self-inflated,
Does not behave indecently to shock,

It does not look for its own interests,

Does not become incensed.
It does not keep a count of wrongs,
It does not get glad through revenge.

But is gladdened when the truth prevails.
Bears, believes, and hopes all things,
Love never gives up, it always works through,
To outlast and outlive, to endure all things."

There are other places in the Bible too, that give
a wider view.
Like love that cares what the Creator thinks,
Things in harmony with that, we're happy to do.

And for example, there's no fear in love.
Yes, love throws fear outside.
Love builds others up, it's true,
Love is born for trying times.

It's a fruitage of the Holy Spirit,
Which we don't have in and of ourselves.
So when we find ourselves lacking in it,
We can just ask, and get the Book down off the
shelf.

And I'm reminded of Shakespeare's take,
By the old Hebrew word for loyal love,
It doesn't alter when it alteration finds,
Nor bends with the remover, to remove.

With another's best interests in our hearts
We attach ourselves to a person, purpose or
place,
We don't let go, we see a good intention through,
No matter what it takes.

And so far, the facets that I can count,
Come to 26 or thereabouts.
And so I say, love is a like
A pre-cut multifaceted diamond, a rare jewel to
be found.

When A Way Forward Feels Right

When a way forward feels right
The drive is always there
When an idea strikes or inspiration hits
You can't help but bring it to bear.

When a way forward feels right
You don't even need to wait
For timing to be perfect,
Nor for all the puzzle pieces to fit.

You just go with the feeling,
You just go with the flow.
You just know it'll work out ok,
The details, you don't need to know.

So if you're not feeling motivated
Or not clear on what to do next...
It's ok, try honing in on the feeling.
Keep looking for what feels right, what feels
blessed.

Anger Can Become A Comfort Zone

Anger can become a comfort zone
When we feel wronged,
When we feel loss,
When we feel pain.

It helps our nervous system feel
In control,
or soothed,
'Til at peace again.

Yet control is an illusion.
Not real,
Not truly
What's going on.

We actually only have two options,
Out of which we only get to choose one.

You can see life as happening to you,
Or see you as happening to life.

And when you choose the latter,
You can choose to respond with kindness.

The truth is that we need each other,
And anger pushes people away.
It's ok sometimes, we understand,
But not as a comfort zone in which we choose to
stay.

Because anger can only get us so far,
While kindness paves the way…
For better results in the long run,
And happiness even now, wouldn't you say?

No Place To Hide

Why does the body shake,
When we laugh or when we cry?
When we're scared out of our boggled minds,
And the stakes feel really high?

Do emotions have an electric charge?
To bodies then, electrify?
When our bodies find it just too much,
Do tremors personify…

The inner fears, anxiety,
The body-racking sobs that speak…
Articulating words we didn't know,
And thoughts we dared not think?

Then laughter comes along to join,
The jolly rollercoaster ride…
Of human emotions, fully charged,
Through whose shakes, offer no place to hide.

Each Step Forward

If you knew you only had a day
What would you choose to do?
If you could get somewhere in an instant,
And not have anything to prove?

Or let's say you have a week,
How does your 'to do' list grow?
Who would you choose to spend time with,
Where would you choose to go?

Now let's broaden things a bit,
With a month, or two or three,
And if you had a year or five,
What then, would the difference be?

Let's figure out whats important to you.
It's ok if you're not sure yet.
But let's work so that each step forward,
Is a step you won't regret.

Unboxed

Introvert or extrovert
For years they've made us choose
All these personality tests…
Always give us things in twos:

Introvert versus Extrovert
A Finisher versus Opener
A Realist versus Idealist
A Feeler versus Thinker.

But here's a "what if" to think about,
What if we're capable of both?
What if we're capable of all of them?
In all sorts of measures, and modes?

I believe we are, indeed, it's true,
Though it's ok to "find ourselves" in some.
Some of the types we relate to most,
And we're glad to find like-minded ones.

But from there let's spring board further,
Into our deeper selves.
I believe we're more complex,
Than for years, these tests have held.

I take each question on these tests,

Qualify them by a factor of at least ten.
I answer most of them by saying to myself,
"It's not as simple as that, it depends…"

Take for example this question:
"Do you usually speak your mind?"
I say: "It depends… if with someone,
Who puts me on guard, or with a trusted friend."

And so it goes with all of them,
I use the questions to find,
A way into my deeper self,
A way to explore my own mind.

I love understanding the way we work,
The way we humans tick.
I've been fascinated by these tests,
Since I was ten and six.

So I listen out for the chiming of
Mine and other's hearts' clocks.
While personality tests may hem us in,
My own method helps unbox…

The many facets of ourselves,
Our learned and natural skills.
Which then, we direct and apply into,
Jobs that help pay the bills.

This method is the first of its kind
To link your stories to your strengths.
The first to help you frame them that way,
Which empowers you, to no end.

If you're worried, the Bardette ™ method
Will puff you up or turn you cocky, even,
Don't worry, it hones in on inner treasures,
Which are key to a humble confidence.

Those inner, treasured memories, buried,
Often hold the key that unlocks…
Your ability to know your worth and see,
Your favourite, unique self, unboxed.

A Way Back to You

All of us feel lost sometimes,
All of us, confused.
Figuring out, who we are
Can be a little fear inducing.

Who wants to look inward,
Who wants to find the truth,
Who wants to know what's hiding there,
Afeared they'll find nothing good?

But that's why I'm here to say to you,
That good you'll surely find.
I want to help reassure,
And convince you it's worth your time.

You'll find a way back to you,
Find things you forgot were there.
Find inner treasures, inner stores,
You always had in you, to be fair.

The Resonant Resume™

"Customer personas"
"Client avatars"
Understanding 'psychographics'
'People from venus, people from mars'

'How to attract your ideal client'
'How to hone in on your voice'
All of the ways to market ourselves
All of the "B2B"/"B2C" advice!

Curious that no one is flipping it
For us job seekers selling our skills
'How to attract your ideal employer'
Convince them to help pay your bills!

Through your unique voice and expert
messaging
You can cut through the fray and the noise
Your Resonant Resume™ would resonate right
Your interviews, you'd own with your poise!

I'm going to start calling it
Individual-to-Business marketing
A skill we shy job seekers need
It's unfair that's the case, if marketing's not what
we do,

But desperate times call for desperate deeds

So I'm here to help coach you through it
Here bringing optimism to your days
You don't have to go it alone you know,
Bardette can help you craft resonant resumes!

You'll Always Find What You're Looking For

Let's face it, we all have an ego
And we like it when we get things right.
So how ironic it is, when we feel of no worth
We'll find confirmation anywhere in sight.

It'll look for proof that we're of no use,
Rack up all the reasons that we were never
Chosen or seen, so when we're falling apart,
Our ego helps us keep it together?

It soothes us to think, that we know why we feel,
So down, so useless, so low.
But what if that's all just a ploy, and a need
That we're filling, that of, our ego?

Is it possible to flip the story?
And find other reasons for our feeling so bad?
Outside of ourselves, outside of this realm?
Outside of stories we tell ourselves in our heads?

Answering that, we can look for different proofs.
Proof that this world was made for you.
The sun that gives light, the air that gives life,
The water that keeps coming back, new.

Those are just three proofs that we are loved,
Long before we entered the scene.
It's less to do with us than we think, same can be said
For wrongs done to us, the state the world is in.

So I get it when you feel low, but just remember
You'll always find what you're looking for.
It comes down to the fact that we like to be right.
Proofs your loved? Tune your love radar, to find more.

Shattered, Then Put Back Together

Have you ever been shattered, then put back
together
By something so simple as music?

If it's just the right kind, it'll paint cracks that it
finds,
In your heart, gold: the art of kintsugi.

Make Friends With Mind-Blank Moments

I just thought of
The perfect thing to have said,
Why couldn't I think of it then?

Why does my brain do that to me?
When the moment's already gone?

And when…

That perfect thing seems
No longer relevant,
And I no longer am afforded,

The chance to say that perfect thing
The opportunity, aborted.

What if, if only, we'd give our brains the chance,
To do us this favor ahead of time,
To think ahead, and stump ourselves, sooner,
rather than later,

And find…

A way to make friends with mind-blank
moments,
And our brain's ability to make a great come
back.
To make peace with not having all the answers,
The first time around, the first try, the first crack.

Counting Friends to Count On

Tell me about your support system
Tell me about the ones you know
You know you can always count on
The ones who always show

Up for you when it really matters
But also when it doesn't matter much
The ones you can laugh and joke with
Who don't have to say a thing even, when it can
be said with a simple touch.

The ones who can tell just by looking
And who give what it is that you need,
When not everything's quite right in your world,
and they don't,
In return, ask or expect anything.

But maybe you feel that of these you have none.
And maybe that's a painful thought.
But would you be surprised it's a common
thing?
Much too common than it really ought

To be, sadly, it's true that most have few

They can count on in times of distress,
And many have said they can count on one hand
The friends that they can count on, through the
tests…

Through the trials that life can bring, in these
we can see who chooses to stick
Around and by our side, through the fray.
Through the thin, the thick.

The sieve of life gives us clues, to true
friendships, saying,
"It's ok if you don't have many."
So set out like a pioneer heading west,
And be a friend today, to another, to any.

Jack of All Trades

What does it mean to be a jack of all trades,
And master of none, as Shakespeare said?
He went on to say it's better than being
just a master of one, and therefore I beg…

To ask us all to remember that last part,
as often as we remember the first.
And yet I disagree that the two should be
compared,
as if one is better or worse.

The truth is, we all need each other,
and the balance of both is the thing.
The specialists, we turn to when in special need,
while generalists can guide a project to a win.

And if we find ourselves in one box or the other,
Think of times when the relative opposite may
have been true,
Because I believe that we all have it in us,
To rise up to each challenge, anew.

You have it in you to be one, or both of them
together.
If you think you're no good at lots of things,
could you be wrong?

And if you've specialised in one thing your
entire life,
there's still time to start in a new one!

We Will Get There In The End

There's a lot of corn among the lines herein
But I have to say, "Long live the corn!"
This will have been my very first book,
Perhaps you should have been forewarned.

That I'm quirky and weird, fun-loving too,
And maybe therein lies the why
I find myself oversharing then ashamed
So I pull away then, into my shy.

I tried to be "normal" for a year, you know.
It was funny, even to try.
Just writing the list of the things that I thought,
Made one "normal" brought laughter-ous tears
to my eyes.

I'll save that list for another time maybe.
The point is, I know that I'm weird.
And it's not in some quest to find some level of
success
that I share with you my weird.

But it is my hope, that with this book
Despite all the corn, there'll have been

A line or two that resonates somewhat
And something that makes you feel seen.

Because the job hunt can stink, be like walking
through mud.
And it can seem like the tunnel is long, and can
tend,
To be dark, and we forget there's a light in our
sights,
So I promise, we'll get there in the end!

www.ingramcontent.com/pod-product-compliance
Lightning Source LLC
La Vergne TN
LVHW041243200726
843507LV00013B/2799